How to Give a Good Blow Job

The Ultimate Guide to Learning How to Give Good Head

by Jules Stratton

Table of Contents

Introduction 1

Chapter 1: All about Fellatio 7

Chapter 2: How to Give a Good Blow Job 11

Chapter 3: Different Techniques/Positions of Blow Jobs ...23

Chapter 4: Pointers on Giving Good Head...........................29

Chapter 5: Ways to Avoid Gag Reflex during Blow Jobs.....35

Conclusion..39

Introduction

Making love is an art. You have to know all the proper strokes and movements to achieve a mind-blowing orgasm. Giving a good blow job is an essential part of this sensual art. It may seem easy to do when you watch porn films and try to imitate what they do, but the catch is, it's not as easy as it seems. Giving a good head needs proper technique.

You can say that experience is the best teacher, but it helps to learn technique through research as well. Learning how to give good head is necessary, because sex without a proper blow job is simply incomplete. Men want their manhood to be explored, cuddled, sucked, and loved. A man who doesn't want the exquisite pleasures coming from fellatio is unheard of. If ever there's one, he may have some deep-seated reasons.

Not all women know how to perform a blow job properly. Any woman can insert that turgid organ into her oral cavity and perform the oral act, but not all can satisfy their partners completely. If you want to make sure you're satisfying your partner during oral sex, explore all means to make him enjoy your blow job. The difference between satisfying and merely doing is in the technique.

Learn the proper technique and then apply it in your sexual encounters. The game plan is to learn and apply. If you are willing to be taught, you can surely learn to satisfy your partner's craving for a good head, and your relationship in bed will be all the better.

This book will reveal simple techniques on how to give a good blow job. You will also find tips and pointers to ensure that your fellatio will drive your partner to beg you for more.

Chapter 1: All about Fellatio

Fellatio is another term for blow job. It's the act of sucking and licking the penis as a form of oral sex. To perform fellatio, the man can either be sitting, lying down, or standing up. There is no best position, as this will heavily depend on you and your partner's preference. Some men like it standing up because they can control the movement of the woman's mouth more conveniently. Standing up, they usually hold on to the woman's hair or head to guide and control thrusting.

Fellatio is the male counterpart of cunnilingus. Cunnilingus is the oral sex on the female genitalia. Both can be equally satisfying if done properly. Couples who perform the 69 position have experienced incredible sensations brought about only by oral sex foreplay.

The first thing that you must remember as a woman is that a man's penis is the most sensitive part of his body. It is composed of numerous sensory nerves that can shoot a myriad of sensations up his body. This knowledge will make you understand why you should be extra gentle and careful when handling this superbly sensitive male sexual organ.

Preparations in Giving a Good Blow Job:

1. **Drink a lot of liquids to moisten your mouth.** Hydrate with water or other cool drinks. A dry mouth will only give pain and no pleasure.

2. **Tie your hair in a bun.** Although loosely flying hair can be sexy at times, your hair can get in the way. The strands of your hair can even harm the skin of his penis, so get that long hair out of the way, unless he prefers it hanging around your head.

3. **Keep a tube of lube handy.** Prepare a lube that is safe to ingest in case it is accidentally taken orally. Read the label to make sure it won't cause any harmful side effects. Natural lubes are the best option.

4. **Keep your pubic area neat.** You may want to shave or trim your pubic hair. If your partner is turned on by a bird's nest, then by all means give him what he wants. Just be aware that it can get a bit untidy during sex.

5. **Trust your partner.** Although this is a given, it has to be stressed. Making love and intimacy requires utmost trust both ways.

These are the basic steps you got to do to prepare before your partner arrives. The next chapter will reveal the specific steps and other preparations you must do to give a good blow job.

Chapter 2: How to Give a Good Blow Job

If you want to give a good blow job, you must forget about trying to give good head and instead focus on savoring the experience. It's only in doing this that you can relax and indeed give a good blow job. Quite intriguing, yes? But that's how these things work: when you are enjoying what you do, you make it pleasurable for your partner too.

The focus lies on remembering that the penis is the most sensitive male organ. You must inculcate this in your mind during the whole course of your love-making. That's why if you want to truly hurt a man, aim for his groin. To illustrate a bit more, the penis is likened to the skin of a newly born infant—that's how highly sensitive it is. You can say that it's close to the sensitivity of the skin on your breast; with the penis being just a bit more sensitive.

Before you go down on your man, you must learn how to set the mood and prepare him for his most mind-blowing head yet:

Step #1 – Take a Shower Together

You cannot enjoy a blow job if unwanted odors and grime will hamper the act. Some excitement can be derived from dirty, sweaty bodies cavorting, and you licking his earthly-smelling organ, but these can be unpleasant and possibly prevent you from enjoying the act. Take a shower together and soap his organ GENTLY, as if bathing a newly-born infant. Give it all the tender, loving care it deserves. Note that you can start foreplay in the shower, but don't give him head just yet. Just give his penis gentle massages and caresses, until it's clean, fresh-smelling, and ready for some action.

Step #2 – Start Foreplay but Take Your Time

Don't stick his penis into your mouth right after you get out of the shower. Take your time. More intense orgasms are achieved when both partners make love slowly. You can start foreplay with gentle caresses, some kissing, and petting. You can be organized by starting from the top of his head going down to his toes. As previously mentioned, love is an art, so paint your picture with great care. Kiss the top of his head and then go down to his ears and lick his earlobes teasingly. As in a theater production, proper foreplay sets a perfect stage for a good blow job. Think of the blow job as the final act, and your caresses, the initial teasing acts that lead up to it.

Step #3 – Caress His Penis

While you're raining down his head with small kisses and licks, your hands have to be busy down there. Don't massage it; just caress it. Your touch must be like that of a soft feather just about to touch his skin but not quite yet. Trail his shaft using one finger with a very light, feathery touch. Do it slowly and gently. If you have a feather, it can do the trick of teasing his penis. Applying pressure won't increase the sensations. In fact, it will only do the opposite and reduce it. Hence, refrain from doing this no matter how aroused you may be.

Step #4 – Focus on His Neck Area

Slip your lips down his neck and blow small kisses at the back of his neck. Allow your fingers to travel to his nipples and play with them for a while. While you're kissing every inch of skin on his neck and nape, return your fingers to his penis every now and then. Again, apply light, teasing, and feathery touches to the shaft of his penis. By then, his organ may already be turgid. Don't massage it yet. Maintain the light touch of one or two fingers going up and down his shaft and then onto the crown of his penis.

Step #5 – Go Down to the Chest Area

Lower your mouth sensuously to his chest area. Shower his chest with light kisses, accompanied by a little nibbling and sucking on his nipples. Your hands can travel up to his free nipple and down to his penis. Your touch on his penis must still be light and teasing with no firm contact. Use one or two fingers to do this. Imagine the wind blowing on your face—that's how your fingertips should feel on his penis.

Step #6 – Proceed to the Groin Area

Slowly go down to the groin from the chest with your lips lightly kissing and biting along the way. Lick the area between his legs and the top of his pubis. Start kissing his balls and his perineum area. Don't squeeze or apply pressure. This is part of his penis and these are also extra sensitive to the touch. Put a bit of lube in your hands and start fondling his balls gently. Remember, it can never bring pleasure if you don't do it gently.

Step #7 – Tease His Penis

You can then proceed to his penis. Caress the surrounding areas first, then slowly massage and caress his shaft like touching the skin of a baby. Kiss his thighs while caressing his organ. The lube will make it wet and slippery, which is preferred—the wetter, the better. Your lips can proceed to his feet and toes, if you're inclined to do it. Some men enjoy the pleasure that toe-sucking provides them. Now you can see why you needed the shower before sex.

Step #8 – Play with His Balls

You should now concentrate on his balls and penis alternately. Don't squeeze. Apply gentle caresses, massaging the skin lightly, slowly, and enticingly. Remember how you want your nipples and breast to be caressed; that's how he wants his manhood to be adored. The penis needs lighter pressure than your breast, though. Your nipples can enjoy little teeth but his penis and balls won't. Once again for emphasis: NO TEETH. You must do this step VERY GENTLY. His balls are not lollipops; they're made of ultra-sensitive testicular nerves and tubules that can cause considerable amount of pain when touched carelessly.

Step #9 – Lick the Head of His Penis

Now you're ready to heat it up. Gently lick the crown. Look at him and ask him how he wants it done. Men want to know that you're happy giving them good head. Thus communicate with him, while adoring his crown. Listen to his prompts and follow his lead. Your tongue must suck the crown like it's delicious ice cream, relishing and enjoying the moment. Tell him to relax and just absorb the sensations, as he won't totally enjoy the act if he's tense and worried.

Never allow your teeth to come in contact with his penis. This is quite painful and can turn off your partner. Wrapping your lips around them can prevent this from happening, but don't suck his penis yet. Let him wait in anticipation for his blow job.

Step #10 – Run Your Tongue Gently Up and Down His Shaft

When you feel his crown has received sufficient attention, run your tongue along his shaft. Do it inch by inch, as if mimicking a slow moving, soft feather. Let your tongue travel the length of his shaft down to his balls and then up again, back to his head. Bestow kisses and blow soft curls of breathe into his crown and then back down into his balls. Trace the corners of the crown of his penis with your tongue. Relish every movement of this step and enjoy yourself. Do this several times until he begs for more. Again, take note: do this step tenderly, like touching the skin of a newborn baby. This step will not be enjoyable if you don't remember this essential instruction.

Step #11 – Let Your Hand Back Up Your Mouth

As your tongue runs along his shaft, encircle the base of his penis with the fingers of your right hand. As your tongue moves to his crown, follow the movement gently with your fingers. Don't squeeze but caress the base with light rotating movements. Most men prefer a combination of the two. This is because they often masturbate and the feel of your hands oftentimes stimulates them. When your mouth goes up, your hands follow while it rotates at the base of his penis. When your mouth goes down, your fingers massage downwards too. All these should be done using gentle and light touches.

Step #12 – Take His Penis into Your Mouth

Your mouth must contain sufficient moisture to lubricate his penis. Take note that a dry blow job is painful, so get your salivary juices going. Start slowly by taking his crown first into your mouth and then sucking it. Re-apply lube at the base so you can lightly massage it with your fingers, while moving your mouth in and out of his manhood. Blow soft kisses into his crown and then lick and suck again going downwards. Suck gently and lightly because this area doesn't tolerate heavy pressure and deep massaging. The areas that you can give the most pleasure to during oral sex are the underside of the length of his shaft, because it's where the *corpus spongiosum* is found; the balls, and the head of his penis.

Step #13 – Massage the Taint in the Perineum Area

The taint is the area between his anus and his balls. Massage this spot while licking and sucking his penis, and he'll savor the pleasurable sensation. Most men go crazy when you do this. While you massage this area, go up and down his penis with your mouth. Imagine your mouth serving as your vagina. Thus, the grip of your mouth must be similar to that of your vagina—moist and slick.

Step #14 – Doing Deep Throat Penetration

This is a bit difficult for those still new to giving head. The secret is to ease into a deep throat by relaxing your mouth. Don't try too hard. You can always gain that expertise as you perfect the technique of giving head. Open your mouth wide and relax your oral cavity. Slowly take in the length of the penis, inch by inch. Take in only what you can so as not to make yourself gag. There will always be a next time.

Step #15 – Relish the Moment

Don't be in a rush. Relish his penis inside your oral cavity. Lick the shaft while you suck on his crown. Slide his penis in and out of your mouth as you taste every inch of him. Run your fingers around his balls and his taint. Savoring each movement is like drinking a bottle of an old sweet wine, you'll have to do it SLOWLY and GENTLY.

Step #16 – Do Coitus and Fellatio Alternately

To increase the exquisite sexual sensations, you can copulate and do fellatio alternately. You will both need to control your orgasms. Don't fret though because the intensity of your orgasms will be worth the wait. Give him a blow job, and then ride him. When you feel he's coming, withdraw. Tap his penis to give it some air and then go down on him again with your mouth. You can't imagine the pleasure this gives until you experience it yourself.

Step #17 – Swallow His Love Juices when He Orgasms

In fellatio, the incredible sensation of orgasm is diminished when your mouth releases his penis when he comes. If you intend to let him experience the ultimate pleasure of a blow job, then allow him to spew his semen into your mouth. This will heighten the sensation and will make him feel more loved. Some men are turned off when a woman removes her mouth just before ejaculation.

These are the basic steps of giving a good blow job. Men may not attain orgasm through oral sex all the time however, this doesn't mean you did poorly. You can always employ the most common method, the hand-and-suck method, described above.

Follow these steps to give your partner a superb blow job. One cannot stress enough that you should always remember to treat a man's delicate and sensitive penis as gently as you can. This makes the difference between a poor blow job and a good blow job.

Chapter 3: Different Techniques/ Positions of Blow Jobs

As couples become more intimate with each other, they learn to read each other's pleasure cues. They then adjust and customize how they do blow jobs to increase satisfaction. Others like to keep it fresh by trying a new or different technique. Surprise your partner with any of the below variations that will certainly enrich your sex life:

1. **Tongue Squeeze Blow Job**

    This technique involves taking his penis all the way into your mouth and then pushing the head against your top palate, so that the tip rests gently on the roof of your mouth. With your tongue, massage the length of the underside of his penis. Do this if the entirety your partner's penis can fit in your mouth, otherwise you'll gag. If there's no fit, forget about it and just appreciate the other enormous advantage you can gain with his huge penis.

2. **Cream Blow Job**

    Spread some whipped cream on your man's penis and eat it by licking and sucking. Cold cream can add thrill to the sensual act. Ascertain though that your man wants it too and that he's not allergic to any of the ingredients. You may want to try eating cake or pastries too. You can be as creative as your imagination allows. Challenge your mind and devise ingenious ways to give your man pleasure.

3. Kneeling Blow Job

This is a common position that a lot of men are fond of. With your partner standing, you go on your knees to give him a blow job with a combination hand and suck method. This puts your man in the dominant position, and men love it when they can feel empowered.

4. Advanced Blow Job

This is done with you lying down on the bed in a supine position, and your head positioned at the edge of the bed. You can bend your knees to provide easy movement. Your partner stands on the floor with his penis right into your mouth. You can give him an awesome blow job from that position. He can return the favor also by bending forward towards your vagina, where he can suck your clitoris. It's similar to the 69 position but with some modification on the positions.

5. Jack Hammer Blow Job

For this style, you are seated firmly on the floor. Your knees should be bent and your hands firmly planted at your sides. Your man stands and positions his penis directly above your mouth where you can suck and lick it. He has full control of the act, so make sure you're ready for the onslaught of the jack hammer.

6. Plumber Blow Job

You're lying down with your knees bent. Your partner is on all fours with you in between his legs. Your mouth should be directly below his penis so you can suck and lick him. You can hold on to both of his legs as you give him good head. He can reach out to kiss you or touch you.

7. Face Fuck Blow Job

You're lying down on your back with your legs straightened. Your man straddles your face between each leg and proceeds to a kneeling position. You elevate your head using a pillow and give him a blow job from there. This is another dominant position for your man.

8. Intermediate Blow Job

This is similar to the 69 blow job position. There's a little modification, where you're both lying on your sides and giving oral sex to each other. This can give you both incredible ecstasies because you're simultaneously pleasuring each other through your mouth.

Apart from the above examples, there are a number other ways you can give a breathtaking blow job. The important thing is to be attentive to what your partner likes. Be ready to tell him what you like most, too. This will help you experiment and discover what pleasures you and your partner most.

Chapter 4: Pointers on Giving Good Head

Let the following points serve as your guide in giving your man a blow job that will make him feel absolutely special.

1. **Foreplay is just as important**. Foreplay must come with a blow job. Don't go directly to fellatio. This makes the final consummation of the act more pleasurable.

2. **Perform fellatio like a toothless woman.** Let me emphasize this some more: your teeth are not needed, so make them disappear.

3. **Communicate with your partner**. Ask him what he prefers and express your needs too. Partners who learn how to express their sexual needs are happier and more fulfilled than those who don't.

4. **Don't worry if you can't take it all in**. You may not be able to take his entire penis into your mouth. This doesn't indicate that you didn't do a wonderful job. You have your fingers to caress the portion that is left out, so make use of them as well.

5. **A combination of gentle strokes and light sucking is ideal for a blow job.** Use your hands and mouth simultaneously to give your man incredible orgasms.

6. **Maintain eye contact.** Look your man in the eye whenever you can while giving him a blow job. This will make it more erotic and sensual.

7. **Don't think of oral sex as dirty.** Some women can't perform oral sex because they think of the act as dirty. If you're one of these women, you have to change your perception and welcome oral sex as a perfect way to show devotion and love to your partner. It's extremely intimate and it demonstrates complete trust and love between couples.

8. **Use sex toys.** Try using sex toys along with your blow job. Agree on an item that you think can intensify his blow job experience. There are various sex items that can help you stimulate his pleasure points. It's preferable to make use of your hands and mouth, though, because the close encounter will further your intimacy with each other.

9. **Experiment with various techniques**. There's excitement and adventure when you're both ready to explore and experiment. And there's also a possibility that you may be able to add to the various blow job techniques mentioned here.

10. **Slow down when he eventually orgasms.** Let him enjoy the experience fully by slowing down. Allow your touch and caresses to linger as he trembles in the throes of his orgasm. This will prolong the orgasm and intensify the pleasurable sensation.

11. **Be enthusiastic**. Every man wants a lively and passionate sex partner. Your enthusiasm will rub off on your partner, and the act will serve as a physical and spiritual communion between you. This attitude will also be considered sexy as you go down on him.

12. **Feel sexy and confident.** Your confidence is reflected in the way you carry yourself. The reason why some beautiful women lack charm is because they don't feel sexy. Believing in yourself will improve your sex appeal, and when you feel sexy, giving a good blow job is no problem.

13. **Let your partner honestly evaluate you.** Allow your partner to assess your performance. What better way to know how you fared but from your partner himself? Be ready for his feedback and be willing to accept it. This will greatly impact your future sexual encounters and strengthen your relationship.

14. **Beware of sexually transmitted diseases (STDs).** Be sure that your partner is free from STDs before engaging in intimacy. The soft lining of the mouth, when damaged, is susceptible to the invasion of causative agents of STDs. Be judicious with your sex partners and stay safe.

15. **Shave your pubic hair regularly.** This is more hygienic and stops hair from getting in the way— unless your partner prefers it hairy. You can also request him to shave his too. If he doesn't want to, don't force the issue. Don't allow a little hair to ruin your day.

16. **Don't perform fellatio simply for favors.** There are some women who only perform oral sex when their partners grant them favors. This is some sort of emotional blackmail, which is not good for any relationship, and might even destroy it gradually. Sexual acts should never be done as payment for favors granted. This is not what good relationships

are made of. You should make love because you care for each other.

17. **Use both your hands, your tongue, and mouth on erogenous zones**. Go in and out; round and round; and up and down when giving a blow job. Use your different body parts as much as you can to please your partner as much as possible.

These are useful tips you can follow to heighten and enjoy your blow job experience. If at first you don't seem to succeed, don't give up because practice makes perfect. Keep following the techniques here and eventually you'll gain success.

Chapter 5: Ways to Avoid Gag Reflex during Blow Jobs

One of the most common problems when giving a blow job is gag reflex. This is a natural response of the body when something is stuck in the throat. However, it's a turn off for men when you gag during blow jobs. Thus, it's vital that you learn how to control this as much as you can. Some women can control their gag reflex through practice. You can learn to control it too in the long run. So while you're perfecting your blow job technique, here are some ways to avoid gag reflex.

1. **Condition yourself mentally**
   Tell yourself that you won't gag, and imagine yourself performing a deep throat blow job without gagging. Keep this visualization in mind. Relax your throat muscles and inch your partner's penis slowly into your mouth.

2. **Use of numbing drugs**
   This can have adverse effects, so use this cautiously. If you decide to apply numbing agents, be aware that your partner might feel the same numbing effect too. Make him wear a condom for protection. Make sure to discuss this option with your partner before making decisions.

3. **Using your hands to act as an alternative for deep throat penetration**

   You can use your hands to simulate a deep throat blow job. This can be done with your hands massaging and encircling the base of his penis, while your mouth massages its head. The shaft has to be completely covered by your mouth or your hands so that it feels like he's inside your throat.

4. **Practice on bananas or dildos**

   Constant practice will help you stop gagging. Make use of bananas or dildos to do this. Take it slow and don't worry. If you really can't, there are lots of other alternatives. Your partner surely cares more about your comfort.

5. **Breathe through your nose.**

   Learn how to breathe through the nose when giving a blow job. This will help you keep on breathing even if your throat is blocked from taking in air because of your partner's penis. Breathing exercises will help in this process.

6. **Relax your throat muscles**

   Learning to relax your throat muscles will help stop you from gagging. Close your eyes and mentally psyche yourself to relax your throat.

7. **Position yourself so that your throat is parallel to his penis**

    Find a position that allows his penis to be parallel to your mouth. This way you can easily adjust and relax your muscles to allow easier penetration of your mouth. The best position for this is when your head is hanging at the edge of the bed and you're lying supine. He has to be standing up with his penis above your mouth. This is the advance blow job position presented in Chapter 3.

These pointers will help keep you from gagging, but don't despair if you still do. Deep throating can be substituted with many *many* other sex acts that will not hurt you or your partner.

Conclusion

Giving good head is crucial to satisfactory sex. Every man wants to be adored down there, so don't deprive your man of this sensual sensation. It's vital to learn this art of sexual fulfillment—your man wants it just as much as you want to be explored in your love tunnels.

Although some men deny the fact that they want a blow job, your man can never say he's sexually satisfied if you haven't given him a good blow job. So, learn the techniques and pointers here and go ahead and excite him with your new knowledge.

Don't wait for your partner to ask for it. Do it voluntarily and observe how happy it makes him. Show him that you're different from other women, who may have given him head, by using the baby skin touch technique with your gentle fingers and feathery lips. Only women who understand this simple concept can give their partners a superb blow job.

Finally, I'd like to thank you for purchasing this book! If you enjoyed it or found it helpful, I'd greatly appreciate it if you'd take a moment to leave a review on Amazon. Thank you!

Made in United States
Troutdale, OR
09/21/2024